GREATEST WARRIORS
GLADIATORS

ALEX STEWART

FRANKLIN W...
LONDON • SYDN...

First published in paperback in 2014

First published in 2013 by Franklin Watts

Franklin Watts
338 Euston Road
London
NW1 3BH

Franklin Watts Australia
Level 17/207 Kent Street, Sydney, NSW 2000

Produced by Arcturus Publishing Limited,
26/27 Bickels Yard, 151–153 Bermondsey Street, London SE1 3HA

Edited and designed by: Discovery Books Ltd.

Series concept: Joe Harris
Managing editor for Discovery Books: Laura Durman
Editor: Clare Collinson
Picture researcher: Clare Collinson
Designer: Ian Winton

The publisher would like to thank Britannia re-enactment group (www.durolitum.co.uk/) and Deeds of Arms (http://deeds-of-arms.
org.uk/default.aspx) for their assistance in the preparation of this book.
Picture credits:
Alamy: p. 15 (Nick Turner), p. 19 (BlueMoon Stock), pp. 20, 22, 26, 27, 28 (AF archive), p. 23 (The Art Archive), p. 24 (Photos 12);
Arènes de Nîmes – Culturespaces (Marc Fasol): p. 17; Britannia (www.durolitum.co.uk/): p. 4 (Dan and Matt Shadrake), p. 10r (Dan
Shadrake as a Thracian; photograph – petewebb.com), p. 121 (Stephen Knight as a retiarius; photograph – petewebb.com); Corbis:
p. 25 (Michael Nicholson); Deeds of Arms: pp. 10l, 14, 18; Getty Images: p. 16 (AFP); Shutterstock Images: pp. title, 7, 9, 13 (nito),
p. 5 (S.Borisov), p. 6 (Stanislaw Tokarski), p. 8 (Will Iredale), p. 11 (Only Fabrizio), p. 12r (Thorsten Rust), p. 21 (Iakov Kalinin),
Wikimedia Commons: p. 29 (Acquired by William T. Walters, 1883).
Cover images: Arènes de Nîmes – Culturespaces (Marc Fasol): top; Britannia (www.durolitum.co.uk/) (Dan Shadrake as a Thracian;
photograph – petewebb.com): bottom centre; Shutterstock Images (Iakov Kalinin): background.

A CIP catalogue record for this book is available from the British Library.

Dewey Decimal Classification Number: 796.8'09

ISBN: 978 1 4451 3751 3

Franklin Watts is a division of Hachette Children's Books, an Hachette UK company.
www.hachette.co.uk

Printed in China

SL002498UK
Supplier 03, Date 0614, Print Run 3622

CONTENTS

Extreme entertainment 4

Doomed to die 6

Samnite – the stabber 8

Thracian – the slicer 10

Retiarius – the net warrior 12

Fighting women 14

Horsemen 16

Fight school 18

Amphitheatres of blood 20

Horror hunts 22

Gladiators on water 24

Great gladiators 26

Rise and fall 28

Glossary 30

Further information 31

Index 32

EXTREME ENTERTAINMENT

Gladiators were armed **professional** fighters in ancient Roman times. They entertained huge crowds of bloodthirsty spectators with their fighting skills. In deadly battles, they fought for their lives against other gladiators, condemned criminals and wild animals. The more brutal the combat, the more the crowd cheered.

STABBING SWORD

The word 'gladiator' comes from the **Latin** word *gladius*, which means 'sword'. As well as swords, gladiators used other vicious weapons such as spears and knives.

DEADLY ARENA

Gladiatorial fights usually took place in an **arena**, an area covered with sand at the centre of an **amphitheatre**.

COMBAT VENUES

The first gladiator fights took place in public squares, known as forums. From around 50 BCE, as the violent displays grew in popularity, specially designed amphitheatres went up all over the Roman **Empire**.

COLOSSEUM

The largest amphitheatre in the Roman Empire was the Colosseum in Rome. The vast building could hold 50,000 spectators.

FIGHTING TALK

First gladiators

Rome got the idea of gladiator fights from the Etruscans and Campanians. These were Italian **tribes** living in regions near Rome. They held bloody 'funeral games' (*munera*) to honour their dead. The first gladiator fight in Rome took place in the city's cattle market, the Forum Boarium, in 264 BCE. Decimus Junius Brutus staged the ruthless show in honour of his dead father. Three pairs of slaves were forced to fight, dressed and armed not as Romans – that would be dishonourable – but as **barbarians** from Thrace. The three losers died.

DOOMED TO DIE

Thousands of gladiators fought and died in arenas throughout the Roman Empire. The majority were slaves, criminals or prisoners of war, who were forced into this fearful occupation. Most gladiators received some training, but few survived more than ten fights.

A DEADLY CHOICE FOR SOME

Some gladiators were volunteers who entered the violent profession out of choice. They were usually ex-soldiers, or very poor people. They chose to give up their freedom in return for regular meals and a chance of fame, glory and prize money in the arena.

DESTINED FOR THE ARENA

As Rome's empire grew, many thousands of prisoners of war were taken. The captives were often forced to fight as gladiators for the Romans' entertainment.

BLOODY BUSINESS

Gladiators could be bought and sold by wealthy Romans, like houses or slaves. A trained and experienced fighter was very expensive – costing perhaps 1,000 *denarii,* which was more than three years' wages for an ordinary Roman. And very occasionally a good (and lucky) gladiator made a fortune. **Emperor** Nero (ruled 54–68 CE) rewarded Spiculus, his favourite gladiator, with a fine house and rich estates.

DEATH ON THE SAND

A gladiator's training included preparation for an honourable death. Gladiators were not expected to ask for mercy or cry out.

COMBAT STATS

A risky profession

- **Risk of death:** Gladiatorial fights did not always end in death. When entering the arena, gladiators faced about a 1 in 4 chance of being killed.

- **Worst chance of survival:** The *andabata* was a gladiator who fought blind. His helmet had no eye-holes and covered his head completely. He was about 99% sure to die.

- **Number of fights:** Very few gladiators had long careers. Flamma, one of the best, had 34 fights, 21 wins, 9 draws and 4 losses.

- **Average age:** Most gladiators died aged between 18 and 25.

- **Longest lived:** One retired gladiator survived to the age of 90.

SAMNITE — THE STABBER

Gladiators were divided into different types, depending on their armour, weapons and fighting styles. Some of the earliest gladiators were known as **Samnites**. They were named after the tough mountain people of Samnium, who were at war with Rome in the 4th century BCE.

SAMNITE
Early Roman gladiators equipped themselves like Samnite warriors.

STABBING SWORD
A Samnite's main weapon was a straight stabbing sword (*gladius*) about 70 cm (27 in) long.

LEG ARMOUR
Metal leg armour known as a **greave** protected a Samnite's lower left leg.

DEFENSIVE SHIELD
A Samnite carried a large rectangular shield, called a *scutum*, to defend himself.

THROAT-DIVIDERS

Advancing behind his large shield, a Samnite tried to close with his opponent and then strike with his stabbing sword. The best target area was the face or neck – a good hit there ended the fight straightaway. That's how the Samnite's sword got its grim nickname, the 'throat-divider'.

CRESTED HELMET

Samnites wore crested metal helmets. These protected their heads, and made them look taller.

ARM PROTECTION

A Samnite protected his sword arm with a guard called a *manica*. The *manica* was a common piece of armour used by many gladiators.

FIGHTING TALK

A gladiator's fate

A fighter could surrender by raising a finger to the referee. His fate was then decided by the umpire or the crowd. Contrary to popular belief, if the crowd gave a gladiator the thumbs down, he was allowed to live. Thumbs up meant sword raised – death!

9

The people of Thrace were famous in the ancient world for being wild and daring fighters. Some of their soldiers had fought with Alexander the Great (356–323 BCE), the amazing Macedonian general whose army was never defeated in battle. The Romans loved having gladiators named after such successful warriors.

CURVED SWORD

Thracians were lightly armed. They wielded curved swords with blades about 34 cm (13 in) long. The swords were short but they were good for slicing opponents.

THRACIAN SHIELD

A Thracian carried a small square or round shield called a *parma*.

THRACIAN HELMET

Most impressive was a Thracian's helmet. The helmet had a wide brim and a visor to cover the face. It was decorated at the top with a mythical bird called a griffin.

GREAVES

A Thracian's leg armour covered the whole of his legs, up to the thigh.

IMPERIAL FAVOURITES

The Thracians were the favourite gladiators of Emperors Caligula (ruled 37–41 CE) and Trajan (ruled 98–117 CE). It is said that when Caligula became emperor he rode across a specially built bridge to his throne – dressed as a Thracian gladiator!

EMPEROR TRAJAN

To celebrate his victory over the Dacians, Emperor Trajan held a festival that included wild animal fights and gladiatorial contests. It is thought that around 5 million spectators came to see the violent displays.

COMBAT STATS

Emperor's celebrations

Following the defeat of the Dacians in the Danube region, Emperor Trajan celebrated back in Italy with 123 days of brutal partying (107 CE).

- **Gladiator fights:** 10,000 gladiators took part in gladiatorial contests as part of the celebrations.

- **Animal deaths:** 11,000 dangerous wild animals, such as lions and bears, were killed during the festival.

RETIARIUS — THE NET WARRIOR

The *retiarius*, or net fighter, was one of the lowliest of all gladiators. Equipped like a fisherman, he wore hardly any armour and entered the arena with just a net and a three-pronged trident.

NET

The *retiarius* relied on a net to entangle his opponent before jabbing him with his trident.

ARM AND SHOULDER GUARD

A *retiarius* wore no helmet, but one arm and shoulder was protected by armour.

THREE-PRONGED TRIDENT

A *retiarius* carried a long, three-pronged spear or trident. He used it to keep his opponent at a distance while trying to trap him in the net.

LIGHT FEET, QUICK ARM

Nimbleness was the key to success as a *retiarius*. Without a shield or helmet, he had to be quick on his feet to stay out of trouble. *Retiarii* usually fought against heavily armed gladiators, such as **secutores** or **murmillos**.

SECUTOR

Secutores, or 'chasers', were specially trained to fight against *retiarii*. They wore helmets as well as arm and leg protection, and they carried a shield and a stabbing sword.

FIGHTING TALK

The fish-man

The *retiarius'* deadliest foe was the *murmillo*, or fish-man. The name came from the fish-style crest on the *murmillo's* helmet. This odd-looking gladiator had an arm guard, leg and feet guards, and a large rectangular shield. His weapon was a stabbing sword. *Murmillo* vs *retiarius* was one of the crowds' favourite fights, with the fish-man often coming out on top.

FIGHTING WOMEN

By the 1st century CE, gladiatorial contests had become lavish, weird and horrible. They featured wild animals, dwarves, children and women. Throwing females into the arena was seen as something special.

NOVELTY ACTS

In Roman eyes, fights between females made an unusual change from contests between male gladiators. Women were made to battle with wild animals or put on armour and hack at each other like male gladiators.

TWO-AGAINST-ONE

Women gladiators usually fought each other, not men. Sometimes they had to fight in two-against-one contests like this one.

WOMEN WARRIORS

Like male fighters, most female gladiators were slaves or prisoners of war. Scholars believe that they were trained to fight, but not in the all-male gladiator schools. They usually fought with swords and shields, and wore arm protectors and greaves on the lower leg. They were rarely given the protection of a helmet.

BATTLE REPORT

Imperial nasties

The cruellest shows seem to have been organized by the emperors themselves. In 66 CE Nero organized a massive battle between two groups of men, women and children. Twenty three years later, in the time of Emperor Domitian, a battle was arranged between an army of women and an army of dwarves. We do not know who won.

HORSEMEN

Gladiatorial contests mirrored combat on the battlefield. Just as armies had **cavalries**, there were mounted gladiators who fought on horseback. These horsemen, or *equites*, were the cream of the gladiators.

A FAIR FIGHT
To make for an even fight, *equites* only fought each other. The battles began on horseback but usually ended on foot.

SHIELD
Equites carried shields about 46 cm (18 in) in diameter.

BATTLE HORSE
In Roman times, a good horse cost as much as a new family car costs today. They were ridden without **stirrups**, which had not been invented.

ENTER THE BRITS

After conquering Gaul (France), in 55 and 54 BCE Julius Caesar came to Britain. Here his soldiers found a new weapon, the war chariot. Before long, gladiators (known as *essedarii*) were fighting each other from chariots back in Rome. Because horses and chariots were costly, these thrilling gladiatorial contests were the most expensive of all.

FIGHTING TALK

Deadly chariots

There are reports of some of Rome's enemies using 'scythed chariots' – chariots with knives sticking out of the axels on either side. We do not know for sure whether scythed chariots were used in the gladiatorial arena – but if so, they would certainly have made the shows more gory!

FIGHT SCHOOL

Gladiators were professional fighters who were expected to put on a good show. To guarantee this, from 105 BCE, they trained in special gladiator boarding schools. Here, a gladiator learned to fight with skill – and to die bravely.

WEAPONS TRAINING

Gladiators were given training in different fighting styles and techniques. Students practised with wooden or blunted weapons.

TOUGH TRAINING

At school, most gladiators lived and slept under guard so they could not escape. They were fed a special high-energy vegetarian diet of cereals and dried fruit, and given top-level medical attention, including regular massage. Each group of gladiators (*familia*) was trained by a manager (*lanista*) who could hire them out for a good price.

READY FOR THE ARENA

No owner wanted to lose one of his valuable gladiators. Trainees were ready to enter the arena only when they had proven themselves skilful enough to reach the top grade (*primus*).

FIGHTING TALK

A gladiator's oath

On becoming a gladiator, a recruit swore this oath: 'I promise to endure to be burned, to be bound, to be beaten, and to be killed by the sword.'

AMPHITHEATRES OF BLOOD

The earliest Roman amphitheatre was built of wood in about 110 BCE. Larger stone amphitheatres followed and eventually there were amphitheatres in some 230 important towns and cities all over the Roman Empire.

BLOOD AND SAND

Amphitheatres were usually oval in shape. They had tiered seating so every spectator had a good view. At the centre was the arena, a word that comes from the Latin *harena*, meaning fine sand. The sand on the floor of amphitheatres helped to soak up the blood. On games days, pine cones were burned in special holders around the arena. The strong, sweet smell hid the stench of blood and gore.

ANCIENT SITE OF SLAUGHTER

The Colosseum in Rome, shown below, is now partly in ruins, but it remains an impressive symbol of Roman imperial power. For hundreds of years, this immense building served as the venue for Rome's spectacular gladiatorial contests, and it was here that many thousands of gladiators and animals met their deaths.

ANCIENT ARENA

The original flooring of the Colosseum, which has now collapsed, was laid over the stone and brick passages running underneath it.

COMBAT STATS

The Colosseum

- **Date of construction:** begun 72 CE, finished 80 CE
- **Opening celebrations:** 100 days of gladiator fights
- **Maximum capacity:** 50,000 spectators
- **Wild animals slaughtered:** 9,000 in the 100-day opening celebrations alone
- **Most gladiators in one event:** 10,000 in 123 days of contests = 81 gladiators per day for half a year
- **Total number of people to die in the Colosseum:** 500,000 (estimated)

HORROR HUNTS

By the time of the first emperor, Augustus (ruled 27 BCE–14 CE), gladiatorial displays usually included mock animal hunts. Wild beasts were brought to Rome from Africa, Asia and Europe. The animals were slaughtered as a gory warm-up before the main event.

BEASTS FOR SLAUGHTER

Exotic creatures were particularly popular with audiences. The animals killed in Roman arenas included bears, snakes, panthers, giraffes, crocodiles and elephants.

TIGER ATTACK
A fully grown tiger was more than a match for an armed man.

CONDEMNED TO THE BEASTS

Fully trained gladiators were rarely asked to fight animals. The usual beast-fighters (*bestiarii*) were untrained criminals or prisoners. From around 100 BCE, a common death penalty was *damnatio ad bestias* – condemned to the beasts. Instead of being hanged or crucified, the guilty person was thrown into an arena to be torn to pieces – normally by lions.

BEAST VS GLADIATOR

A Roman mosaic from the 4th century CE depicts a gladiator fighting a wild beast.

COMBAT STATS

Order of play at a gladiatorial display

- **Six weeks in advance:** publicity leaflets and posters
- **Nightfall (7 pm) on day before the contest:** feast for gladiators
- **Sunrise (5 am) on day of contest:** detailed programmes (*libelli*) available
- **Early morning (9-10 am):** procession (*pompa*) into arena
- **Mid morning (11 am):** wild beast hunt
- **Late morning (12 noon):** executions
- **Early afternoon (2 pm):** comedy shows, including mock fights
- **Afternoon (3-6 pm):** gladiatorial fights
- **Evening (7 pm onwards):** female gladiatorial contests
- **Night (around 9 pm):** closing ceremony, music and clearing up begins

GLADIATORS ON WATER

In 46 BCE, the brilliant Roman general Julius Caesar introduced a new kind of gladiatorial contest. This was the mock naval battle or *naumachia*. The show involved real ships, packed with gladiators, fighting each other on a lake or in a specially flooded arena.

BATTLESHIP

Roman warships were powered by sails and, in battle, rows of oars. A **trireme** had about 170 rowers and 60 soldiers on board. The aim was to **ram** an enemy vessel and sink it.

NAUMACHIA

In 42 BCE, Emperor Augustus built this special amphitheatre on the right bank of the River Tiber for naval battles. It was approximately 533 x 355 m (580 x 390 yd) and had room for 30 warships with 3,000 fighting men on board.

COMBAT STATS

- **Largest recorded *naumachia*:** staged in 52 CE, by Emperor Claudius (ruled 41-54 CE), on Lake Fucino
- **Number of ships:** 24 full-size triremes (three banks of oars) and 26 **biremes** (two banks of oars)
- **Opposing fleets:** Rhodians (from Rhodes) vs Sicilians, with 2 fleets of 25 ships each
- **Number on board:** 1,900 sailors and warriors, all criminals due to die, with each side commanded by one retired gladiator
- **Size of crowd:** 500,000
- **Battle salute:** before the battle, the competitors said to the emperor '*Morituri te salutant*' - 'Those about to die salute you!'

GREAT GLADIATORS

For some brave and skilful gladiators, success in the arena brought wealth, fame and glory. For a few, it even brought freedom. Great gladiators were as famous in Rome as sports stars are today.

SPARTACUS

Spartacus, played here by Andy Whitfield in the television series *Spartacus: Blood and Sand* (2010), was one of the most famous gladiators of all. His story has inspired people ever since to fight against slavery, cruelty and injustice.

FIGHTING TALK

The greatest gladiator

The Greek soldier Spartacus was sent to a gladiator school. In 73 BCE, he broke out and formed a rebel army of slaves and gladiators to fight against the Romans. Camped on Italy's Mount Vesuvius, they defeated several Roman forces sent against them. Eventually, in 71 BCE, they were defeated in the Battle of Sele. Spartacus' body was never found. 6,000 of his followers were crucified.

REWARDS FOR SUCCESS

As well as prize money, a victorious gladiator would be given a crown or palm branch. If he had impressed the spectators with his skill and courage, they would sometimes throw down money for him. After a famous fight that ended in a draw in 80 CE, Emperor Titus gave both the gladiators – Priscus and Verus – their freedom.

HITS WITH THE GIRLS

Roman writers tell us that muscular gladiators were very popular with the women in the audience. The better-looking gladiators were never short of a date, although they had to keep the meetings secret.

CELEBRITY STATUS

Victorious gladiators often had huge numbers of fans, just like the actor Russell Crowe, seen here in the film *Gladiator* (2000).

At the height of their popularity in the 1st century CE, gladiatorial shows were costing around 180,000 *denarii* to put on – that's at least £250,000 in today's money. By the 4th century CE, the Roman Empire was poorer. Attitudes were changing, too, and the games gradually died out.

GLADIATOR COMMODUS

Emperor Commodus (ruled 161–192 CE), played here by Joaquin Phoenix in the film *Gladiator* (2000), was famous for entering the arena himself dressed as a gladiator. He butchered numerous animals, including elephants and giraffes.

SPIRALLING COSTS

The first gladiatorial contests were organized by wealthy individuals. As the displays became more lavish, costs rose and they were largely taken over by the emperors. The shows became part of the government's entertainment programme of public games or *ludi*. They were popular with many Roman emperors, who saw them as a way of winning approval and displaying their wealth and power.

CHRISTIANS IN THE ARENA

By around 100 CE, the Christian religion was spreading across the Roman Empire. Christians, who said gladiatorial fights were murder, were thrown to the lions for refusing to worship the emperor.

AN END TO CRUELTY

Many emperors, starting with Constantine in 325 CE, ordered gladiatorial shows to stop. Their commands were not always obeyed. In 365 CE, Christians were still being thrown to the lions for having an illegal faith. However, after Emperor Theodosius made Christianity the official religion of the empire, gladiatorial games gradually came to a stop.

CONDEMNED TO THE LIONS

A painting by Jean-Leon Gérôme (1883) depicts a group of Christian prisoners who have been condemned to face the lions.

FIGHTING TALK

Emperors in the arena

At least eight Roman emperors – Caligula, Caracalla, Commodus, Didius Julianus, Geta, Hadrian, Lucius Verus and Titus – are said to have fought as gladiators. In fact, they all fought 'staged' fights and never put themselves in real danger. Commodus, who called himself a *secutor*, shot 100 lions from a safe platform and cut the heads off ostriches.

GLOSSARY

Amphitheatre (Meaning 'place for all-round viewing'.) A circular or oval stadium with an arena in the centre.

Arena A sand-covered circular or oval space at the centre of an amphitheatre where gladiators fought.

Barbarian The Roman word for non-Romans (literally 'bearded ones').

Bireme A warship with a sail and two banks of oars on each side.

Cavalry Warriors who fought on horseback.

Denarius A Roman coin (plural *denarii*).

Emperor The head of an empire.

Empire A country or state and all the lands it controls.

Equites The Latin word for cavalry and for gladiators who fought on horseback.

Greave Leg armour.

Latin The language of the Romans.

Murmillo A gladiator with a fish-style crest on his helmet.

Professional Working or fighting as one's job, for pay or other rewards.

Ram To use a large metal spike to smash an enemy ship.

Retiarius A gladiator who fought with a net and trident.

Samnite Someone from Samnium in central Italy; also an early type of gladiator.

Secutor A type of gladiator that was trained to fight a *retiarius*.

Stirrup One of two metal hoops for a horse rider's feet, helping them balance.

Thracian Someone from the region of Thrace; also a type of gladiator.

Tribe A large group of people living together, like a clan.

Trident A lance with three prongs at the end.

Trireme A warship with a sail and three banks of oars on each side.

FURTHER INFORMATION

Books

Guillain, Charlotte. *Gladiators and Roman Soldiers*. Raintree, 2011.

Burgan, Michael. *Life as a Gladiator*. Capstone, 2010.

Watkins, Richard Ross. *Gladiator*. Houghton Mifflin, 2001.

Malam, John. *You Wouldn't Want to Be a Roman Gladiator!* Franklin Watts, 2012.

Websites

Beware – there are many unreliable sites on gladiators.

BBC History: Romans
www.bbc.co.uk/history/ancient/romans/
The best site for young people, from the BBC – historically accurate, with a good piece on the Colosseum. There's a fun game, too!

Roman Gladiators
www.historyforkids.org/learn/romans/games/circus.htm
A simple but child-friendly site. Not a great deal of specific information but a useful reading list at the end.

Gladiator
http://en.wikipedia.org/wiki/Gladiator
This Wikipedia entry is historically accurate and, although written for adults, the language is not too difficult. There are links to dozens of related subjects, such as Samnites.

Gladiators of Ancient Rome
http://legvi.tripod.com/gladiators/id1.html
Another site written with adults in mind – fine for teachers preparing class material of their own. It doesn't contain much that is not in Wikipedia, but the layout is clearer. The sections on topics such as weapons and common misconceptions are most useful.

Index

amphitheatres 4, 5, 20–21
andabata 7
animals 4, 11, 14, 21, 22, 23, 28, 29
arenas 4, 11, 17, 19, 20, 23, 24, 26, 28
armour 9, 14, 15
  murmillo 13
  retiarius 12
  Samnite 8, 9
  secutor 13
  Thracian 10
Augustus, Emperor 22, 25

bestiarii 23

Caesar, Julius 17, 24
Caligula, Emperor 11, 29
chariots 17
Christians 29
Claudius, Emperor 25
Colosseum 5, 21
Commodus, Emperor 28, 29
Constantine, Emperor 29
criminals 4, 6, 23, 25

deaths 7, 11, 18, 21, 22

emperors 7, 11, 15, 22, 25, 27, 28, 29
  as gladiators 28, 29

equites 16–17
essedarii 17

female gladiators 14–15
fish-man 13
Flamma 7
funeral games 5

helmets 7, 12, 15
  murmillo 13
  Samnite 9
  secutor 13
  Thracian 10
horses 16–17

lions 23, 29

murmillos 13

naumachia 24–25
naval battles 24–25
Nero, Emperor 7, 15
net fighter 12–13

oath, gladiator's 19

prisoners 6, 15
prize money 6, 27

retiarius 12–13
Roman Empire 5, 20, 21, 28, 29

Rome 5, 8, 17, 21, 22, 26

Samnites 8–9
schools 15, 18–19, 26
secutores 13, 29
shields 13, 15
  equites 16
  murmillo 13
  Samnite 8, 9
  Thracian 10
slaves 6, 7, 15, 26
Spartacus 26
spectators 4, 5, 11, 20, 21, 27
Spiculus 7
sword 4, 13, 15, 19
  Samnite 8, 9
  Thracian 10

Thracians 5, 10–11
training 7, 13, 15, 18–19
Trajan, Emperor 11
trident 12

weapons 4, 15, 18
  murmillo 13
  retiarius 12
  Samnite 8, 9
  secutor 13
  Thracian 10
women 14–15